WAITING FOR THE ALCHEMIST

OTHER POETRY BY MARK PERLBERG

The Burning Field (1970)
The Feel of the Sun (1981)
The Impossible Toystore (2000)

poems

WAITING FOR THE ALCHEMIST

MARK PERLBERG

LOUISIANA STATE UNIVERSITY PRESS BATON ROUGE

This publication is supported in part by an award from the
National Endowment for the Arts.

NATIONAL
ENDOWMENT
FOR THE ARTS

Published by Louisiana State University Press
Copyright © 2009 by Mark Perlberg
All rights reserved
Manufactured in the United States of America

LSU Press Paperback Original
First printing

DESIGNER: AMANDA MCDONALD SCALLAN

TYPEFACE: MRS EAVES

PRINTER AND BINDER: THOMSON-SHORE, INC.

Library of Congress Cataloging-in-Publication Data
Perlberg, Mark, 1929–
    Waiting for the alchemist : poems / Mark Perlberg.
        p. cm.
    ISBN 978-0-8071-3399-6 (pbk. : alk. paper)
    I. Title.
    PS3566.E6915W35 2009
    811'.54—dc22

                                        2008026612

The author would like to thank the editors of the following journals, in which some
of these poems were first published: *Prairie Schooner:* "Orchids and Eagles," "After a
Sung Dynasty Scroll by Hsiao Chio," "The Return of the Hunters," "The Kitchen
Bird," "The Island without Tourists," "Just Once," "Waiting for the Alchemist,"
"Nameless," "The Reading," "In George Trambas' Body Shop"; *Spillway:* "A Ques-
tion for Eugene Atget"; *Rhino:* "Silence at 5 A.M."; *Free Lunch:* "We Looked at Each
Other on Car 22" and "More"; *Fifth Wednesday:* "Once in a While"; *december:* "Ten
Minutes in Skaneateles, N.Y."

"Orchids and Eagles" and "The Box of Clouds" were published as broadsides by *The
Poetry Center of Chicago.*

Special thanks to the Lannan Foundation for a writer's residence in Marfa, Texas,
where some of these poems were written, and to Hilda Raz, editor-in-chief of *Prairie
Schooner,* for her generous support over the years.

Once again to Anna and in memory of my brother Paul.

CONTENTS

V

I

Orchids and Eagles

Something happened to the cables
that run under miles of water to our island,
so we play cribbage in the light of six candles
and a hurricane lamp.

I look up from my cards. In the black window opposite,
the assortment of candles and the lamp float in the glass,
and I am back in the dining room of a hotel
in Morelia.

Tall white candles and white orchids float in a wall
of wood-framed windows above the valley,
mingled with pricks of light from the old city—
images that have not risen to mind for thirty years.

What is memory? Praise it. Praise its strings and loops
of orchids floating in the night above the old Mexican town—
and yesterday—that pair of eagles, drifting,
floating above the island, dallying with the wind.

After a Sung Dynasty Scroll by Hsiao Chio

The great crag fills the sky.
Three waterfalls drop from cliffs without a sound.
Trails wind through trees. They ascend,
disappear, and reappear. A placid

river flows at the mountain's base, where a servant
ties a flat-bottomed boat to a landing.
He has ferried over a pair of sages,
with their topknots and dark crimson robes.
They talk about the Mandate of Heaven
and read their poems to each other.

Near the summit, temple buildings, their roofs curved up
like wings, stand half hidden behind walls and groves of pine.
Has the boatman ferried the men past the world's edge?
Is this the country beyond death?

The Box of Clouds

I keep a box in my study for things that draw me
and are useful sometimes in adversity.
I keep not one, but three, Indian Head pennies,
and old Chinese coins with circlets and squares
cut in their centers. My foot scuffed them up
in an overblown garden.

I keep stamps in odd colors: moss, mauve,
diamond gray. They looked obsolete
the day they were minted.
Feathers that dropped from the sky,
my airedale's bark, a child's cry.

I keep a fragrance bottle my muse gave me
when I met her in a blue hotel;
and she startled me into remembering
who I am.

Silence at 5 A.M.

VINALHAVEN, MAINE

Eagles have come back to the island.
Osprey are plentiful again. Soon they will climb
and circle in threes and fours, almost out of sight,
tootling to each other. Last night at dusk a cormorant
burst from its strip of water by the stone bridge.

But where are my morning birds that criss-crossed
our backyard summer after summer?
Finches, gold and purple, black-capped chickadees,
flights of anxious waxwings.
Where is the high, sweet, five-note piccolo call
of the white-throated sparrow?

Waiting for the Alchemist

The October sun fires late chrysanthemums,
garnet, lavender, bright yellow.
It strikes an antique dollhouse set down
on the stump of an elm.
A wicker bell tolls.

In my back garden at five in the afternoon,
my shadow's a hundred feet long.
If I squint sidewise, just so, at the white sun
on a day like this,
I might discover the philosopher's stone.

Against Cosmology

I don't care that the universe is fifteen
billion years old.

I don't care that it contains more dark matter
than the leaping zillions of stars,

that there is more empty space
in the universe than anything.

Move close to me. This is our day on Earth
like any other average miraculous day.

The Return of the Hunters

after the painting by Brueghel

They enter the scene under a gray, mottled sky
with their dogs. They have reached the crest
of a snowy hill above their village
after a day of hard slogging.
Dark birds brood on iron-cold branches.
Below, skaters thrust and turn on a frozen pond.

How many times have I looked at this translation
of a world and failed to notice the hunters' game bags
are empty? Even the dogs are dejected.
Winter will be endless.

Monday

Goodbye roses, she said,
bowing slightly toward
two smoky-pink blooms
opening in the morning quiet
of our living room.
Keep the house beautiful
till we return.

II

Song of the Platelets

I

Winter dawn. I raise the shade in my hospital room
above the domes and spires of Chicago. Windy and cold
outside. Steam blowing hard from vents, heeling over
like sails vaporizing away.

My door opens. The masked blood lady.
"Mr. Mark, why you up so early
all the time?"

"I'll need a pressure bandage
when you stick me."

"Yes I know. You a bleeder.
Your platelets is so low."

She slaps my arm below the line
of the blue elastic tourniquet
to bring the blood up.

"Now come platelets—be nice.
We need to get this young man
outta this place for New Years.
Talk to your platelets
Mr. Mark. Talk to them!"

I'm with you, Benina. I'm with you.
I *do* talk to my platelets.

2

Second hour after breakfast, the next huge
event of the morning. My attending will arrive
to tell me the result of the platelet exam;

they must reach 10 before I can go home.
He arrives with a smile and a sharp sharp nose.
Interns, residents, thin, short, white coats,
trail and settle after. They are about to perform
a motet outside my room.

"It is *possible,* sir, we may
have to raise the chemo to a somewhat
more aggressive level."

3

In the gray afternoon a retired rabbi, a volunteer
from the chaplain's office, floats by
like an unmoored canoe.

"May I ask, do you
belong to a congregation?"

"I'm sorry, Rabbi, I'm afraid I'm one of those
Jews still unmoored by the Holocaust."

"Personal experience, sir?"

"Not personal, though never remote."

"Rabbi, tell me, who needs a God
who couldn't/wouldn't protect the six million?"

"But Hashem gave man and woman the world,
said do what you're gonna do with it. Hashem,
God the Merciful, God the Judge; both parts of God.
We know what happened. Read the papers, watch TV.
You know the Shema?"

"Hear O Israel, the Lord our God,
the Lord is One."

"I hate to say this to you Rabbi,"—
such a short man, with a smile, a pot belly
and small gray beard. "I hate to say this:
Even the sublime 23rd is a cop-out, a pipedream.
I ask myself, do I want it read at my funeral?
It's poetry, not promise."

He will lay a table before me
in the presence of my enemies . . .
In the valley of the Shadow of Death . . .
His Rod, His Staff . . .

4

Night. Not a nurse at the station.
I study the digital clock, tossing off my minutes.

Suddenly, a long ago attic in the big brick house
my father built above the river and died in soon after.
Somehow, the house is ours again. I am ten.
I open an attic door and walk out under the eaves.
They are there: trunks, dismantled beds, pictures
turned to the wall, toys, games, my lead soldiers.
No one is home. A night of wild wind, violent rain.

But now the murmur of voices
and low bluish lights in the hall.
Things move by on soft wheels.
They have come back, the nurses.
Soon Benina will come to draw blood again.
It must be close to dawn.

I tunnel myself up, almost to the level
of the holy/unholy psalm.

The Gift

for Anne Dirks, poet

When I came to visit that final time, I was surprised you greeted
me at the door in a red sweater and salt-and-pepper slacks.
I had thought to warm an hour for you at your bedside
with talk of books and new poems.

I was surprised that lunch would be served in the dining room.
You had told me, before we sat down to a cream soup
and plates of salad, that your new helper was a hospice nurse.
I raised a shield against the thought, but her movements,
somber and strong, began to seem certain as death.

You kissed me on the mouth as I was leaving—
a gift for the work we had shared, the gossip and laughter,
and for what was left unsaid. You were untying a thread
that still bound you to the world.

Vital Signs

In a room before surgery, I fix on a print
of *The Hay Wain* over the nurse's shoulder.

Light stipples a country stream where it pools
in front of a house, its stucco crumbling.
Black horses, a man and his wagon
stand in the pool. I hear the horses drinking.
A dog has come down the bank. Head cocked,
he argues with a boy in the back of the wagon.
A boat like one I owned a lifetime ago
lies half-buried in reeds.
Under a skyful of rolling clouds
light spatters a meadow.

I ride the gurney.
High summer buzzes and drones.

A Question for Eugene Atget

What is the girl in your celebrated photograph doing?
The organ grinder is grinding away, his mustachios
and cheery dirty face, his instrument, became a cliché
that conjured Paris in a hundred films.
But the girl, her arms thrown in the air—is she crying
or rapturously singing?
How did the morning go for her, when she followed
the old man as he rolled his cart beyond the border
of the picture?

Interviewing Chagall

I interviewed Chagall over lamb chops
and French peas in a professor's apartment.
A stocky man with a face like Harpo Marx.
Big chest thrust into gray tweed, forest green shirt,
red tie. I was the man from *Time*.

He had flown to my gray city that cold spring
from Provence. He was working in pottery there
and spoke of the elements that make a jar:
fire, earth, air.

I have the book he signed for me *en bon souvenir.*
Two splendid hours. I wanted more.
I wanted him to lift his felt-tip from his pocket
a second time and splash a bird, a clock with wings,
a horse with a sinister smile beside the gift of his name.

Something extra: a talisman, a piece of the mystery.

A Late Birthday

for Ted Kooser

Most of what I know
other people learn
at odd moments,
in this kind of silence
or that. But we had
to reach this shore
to find it.

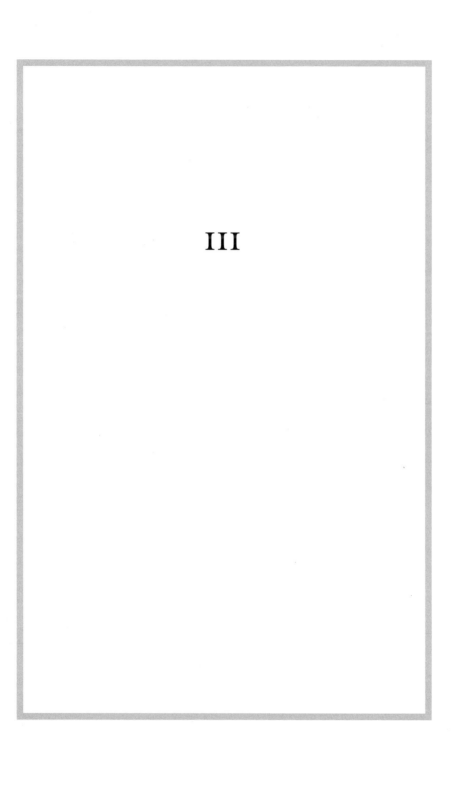

III

Night and Dreams

On nights when I hear you
making small noises in your sleep,
I press my warmth against you
to give you comfort. Fifty years since
you fled Prague and you are having one
of your Nazi dreams.

Men with silver skulls on their caps
are ransacking your house, hunting you down,
and you a girl so small, with brown eyes
and blond braids.

Some nights you are a giant woman with great
muscular arms and wonderful breasts,
breaking each guard in pieces,
freeing all the children who would have died
like your cousin Jana, at seven, in Auschwitz,
but for you.

Nameless

Every family has them.
Photos of people nobody knows,
distant relatives, perhaps,
friends of parents long dead.

A young man poses under the clock
in Prague's medieval square,
shirt open at the neck.
Why the mocking grin?
Wind ruffles his hair.

Saucy in a filmy blouse
a woman bends toward
her photographer
over emptied coffee cups.
Breasts perky as young trout.
Sun, shadows, an outdoor café.

A family strolls in Karlovy Vary.
Solemn, dark-suited father.
Elegant mother with hat and lace gloves.
She holds a child by the hand,
its head encased in bandages.

Snapshots, nothing remarkable,
but my wife dislikes seeing such photos
framed in shops for sale to strangers.

Last night as dusk settled in, she carried
ours in a box to the back garden
and burned them one by one,
in a kind of funeral.
Inside, she lit a yahrzeit candle.

After a Pastel by Seymour Rosofsky

Those Dutch teens in the square—
she in her white Hans Brinker cap
that covers her ears, he in baggy
crimson trousers and yellow shirt.
Why are they talking so calmly
against those slashes of scorched orange?
Can't they see, do they refuse to see
the green man, almost erased, at the edge
of their bench—his wild eyes, his rage?
He knows what brutal wings thrash the air.

Your Dream, My Dream

I

In your dream you are walking in a gray
tattered part of the city.
You pause in front of a broken building,
windows gone, twists of graffiti indecipherable
except for the hate, on dirty brown brick.

Somehow you know the phones are alive.
You walk inside and pick up a phone on a desk.
After decades—my voice on the line.

2

In my dream a phone rings past midnight
in a dark office tower.
Another rings far down the hall. And another.
Phones ring all night in empty offices across the city.
Screeds in colorless ink, sparks flying.

The Reading

ADAM ZAGAJEWSKI IN CHICAGO

He was ill at ease at first.
"Can you hear me? This microphone—"
the *o*'s spoken like the French *u*, with pursed lips.
"Is it better now?"
In a voice that rose and fell, half lyric, half ironic,
came poems of a summer dawn streaked
with odors of mint and dark earth,
of swift rivers hesitantly crossed,
crippled towns, refugees dressed for every season
dragging carts behind them.
And poems studded with abstractions
we teach our students to avoid, like
purity, justice, liberty.

My Muse

I walk up to the checkroom
in the dusky lobby of a blue hotel.
The attendant steps in front of her counter.
She holds out a stringed instrument,
its bowl chipped and painted with smudged
red whorls and gold diamonds.

"Don't you recognize me?
Take this, it's yours."
The air about her ripples a bit
and shines.

Just Once

I have never seen my father
in a dream.
He died when I was five.
A scrap of memory washed
in browns and grays
is all I retain.

If I could see him just once
in my night theater,
what would he say
to his second son
at last?

More

I pin a yellow cottonwood leaf
    on my brown cork board
       and that's the fall.

I keep a chunk of an old oak lobster pot
    with rusty nail holes
       and that's the sea.

I have it from a cardinal, the Roman kind,
    diminishment, too,
       is a form of growth.

Ten Minutes in Skaneateles, N.Y.

A few moments ago the lake was a green satin scarf
with smooth furls for waves and a postage stamp park
for a border. Then the storm struck.
Wind unraveled the scarf to white shreds,
bent curbside saplings over, tore small branches
from trees and flung them onto the grass, while the rain
lashed tardy couples and sent them racing for cover,
drummed on the roofs of cars, boiled in the streets,
hissed against shopfront windows.
Then the storm was over.

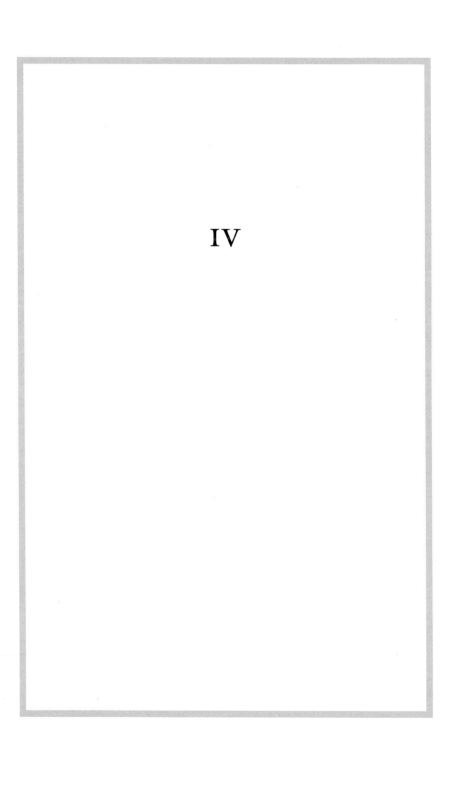

IV

In the Barbershop

My barber, Franco, has no friends.
"All I do is work work work. This is America."
Last fall he closed his shop for a month
and flew to his native town in Catania.

"There I know everybody, they know me.
My wife and I, we walk in the square.
We meet a friend, we sit down, we talk
and have a cappuccino.
Time in Sicily is different from here.
Talk is more important than money.
Do you know the rent I pay for this place?
Where's the leisure, the life?"

All day, as he cuts and shapes
his clients' hair he plays Italian opera.
Casta Diva,
Visi d'arte
Una voce poco fa
Una furtive lacrima.

Pavarotti, the great Domingo, Callas, Fleming,
Bartoli. The music surges, shimmers, dies.
Opera is about large emotions.
It melts his confusions, eases his pain.

At George Trambas' Body Shop

My father died when he was 103.
Every day at noon he sat back, drank
a pint of wine, ate fresh tomatoes
from our fields, maybe a piece of fish,
and napped an hour.
When the Nazis came, they smashed
everything. My father pointed to the sky—
"He'll get it back for us."
My mother died at 63.
The Communists shot my brother.
She could not stop grieving.
The picture on the door?
That's me, in a relay race in Athens.
I was 19, strong, quick. I had promise.
The big man with the mustache,
he was my teacher, a champion.
He went to the villages to look
for talented boys. He taught us
to run and throw the discus.
Of ten brothers, I was the one
who came to the States. My son's a dentist,
my daughter works for the county.
I'm 74. How old are you?

I come here six o'clock, six days a week
for twenty years. Too much work.
Too much responsibility.
I called junk yards all over town
for a left front fender. Your car's *too old*.
But I got one. Maybe they stole it.
I'll try to have the job done by the weekend.
Call me after ten on Friday.
Okay?

Postcards from Crete

1

We climb from our car on a twisting stretch of road
to view the cove below. A tall man—reddish hair
sunburned face—bursts shoeless from his farmhouse,
races after a goat ambling toward the blacktop.
He steams past us, shouts, threatens, claps the goat
over an old stone wall, pauses, straightens his back,
and slowly walks the hundred yards to his house.
Goats, olive trees, cicadas, and the late morning heat.

2

High in the mountains between the Libyan
and Mediterranean seas. No one in sight.
We park at the entrance of a dirt driveway
that disappears behind a hill and walk in a hot wind
toward a church and its dozen graves.
Orchards stipple the coppery mountains.
A large Mercedes pulls around our rented car
and drives past on the road. An elderly couple.
The woman crosses herself as they pass.

3

Our last evening on the island.
Dinner in Rethymnon's Old Town.
Four rows of tables, each with a small
lantern burning. White fish. Crisp cold wine.
The sea laps dark rocks on the beach below.
A ship moves out of the harbor.
Its broad band of stern lights
   dwindles . . .
       blurs . . .
           disappears
in the purple night.

Brothers

We crept out of bed, pulled on swimsuits
and walked the short distance to the beach.
No one stirred in the houses at Hadlock's Cove.
It was an early Sunday morning in a summer
of world war.

Your plan, hatched at night as the white stroke
of a lighthouse swept the walls of our room,
was to slip into Casco Bay, swim the strait
where deepwater ships ran, to Cushings Island.
I was your ten-year-old accomplice. My task:
to keep silent until the time came for bragging,
row the cold blue mile beside you, and fish you
from the water if you tired or developed a cramp.

We made it clear to Cushings. The Army
kept a coast artillery battery there to smash
any Nazi sub rash enough to shadow our great
gray warships in their roadstead down the bay.

We knew the guns' power. On some mysterious
schedule, they fired from a cliff at targets towed
miles out to sea. The boom cracked windows
on *our* island.

We hauled the boat up on a beach, walked past
the loading dock. Why not a look around?
Keeping in shadow, we made our way on a path
to a pair of vast metal doors, camouflage green,
carved in the base of a hill.
The doors stood ajar. Where were the guards?

In the gloom of the cave as far as I could see—
rows of artillery shells, each as tall as I was.
You whispered, "Yellow means high explosive."

What if we struck a spark?
The whole east of Cushings would crash into the sea.
What if we got caught?
Loose Lips Sink Ships.

Creeping close to the ground like men
who would soon appear in a thousand war films,
we slipped back to the punt, rowed home
and never told anybody.

The Old Man in the Green House

His house at the edge of the road is tumbledown,
its siding weathered to a noxious shade of green.
The upper windows, stuffed with stained towels,
clatter in a stiff breeze.
Paper plates cover cracks in the glass.

Summer mornings he sits outside in a nine dollar
plastic chair. Even in August heat he wears a sweater.
Such meals as he has he cooks on an old wood stove,
lifting round iron lids to drop the wood inside.

The town has tried to move him to a trim apartment,
one of a small string built for elders.
He won't hear of it.
The social worker has stopped arguing with him.
"He'll starve to death in there," she says,
"if he doesn't burn up in a kitchen fire first."
But most islanders will push just so far.
Then they wonder who is helping whom.

The Dowser

Take this willow fork in your hand.
Hold it in front of you.
Put your thumbs near the tips of the Y
like this. Now walk toward your well.
If you have the gift, the branch will dip
toward the vein of water.

The willow wouldn't stir for me,
but the dowser thought the slow young man
who drifted across the road
and held out his hand for the branch
might be gifted.
Old now, he needed to give
what he knew away.

The Island Gift Shop

PEAKS ISLAND, MAINE

In summers long past I walked with my grandfather
from his rooms in Merch's cottage to Harry Coxe's
Island Gift Shop.

I made straight for the shelves made to lure small boys
with lobster traps carved to fit my hand, trawlers,
sailboats, tinny ships in bottles.

He purchased cough drops, butterscotch squares,
the latest Agatha Christie or Ellery Queen.

There were watercolors by the Coxe sisters—
Portland Headlight flashing its beam
to warn of sunken cliffs and ridges—
postcards of the sun slipping down past the brown
ferry dock on Diamond Island, souvenir cushions
packed with cedar and pine.

Here comes Mr. Coxe himself! Tobacco-stained teeth,
sinister laugh, and the sisters, tall and wan in pallid colors.
They leap back, astonishing me, as I walk with you
on another island, and the night wind settles about us
a green cloud of cedar and pine.

The Old Inn at Concord

The doors didn't fit their jambs,
the floors rolled out of plumb,
but through the open window
in our room in Henry David's town
a watery breeze poured nightlong
and veil on subtle veil
of insect song.

The Island without Tourists

I

Late September. No more sunsets of lavender,
pale green, rose, soft gray. The west
red-orange like a furnace.

No lights from neighboring houses.
The full moon bright enough to turn the islet
below, each pointed spruce,
upside down in the flat-calm bay.

2

Bright morning. Wind rushes in treetops.
Aerial surf swoops, roughs my hair,
sizzles in my ears.

My own sound in the mix—
big shoes on gravel.
It's all music.

V

In Memory of My Brother

And so they took your ashes to a quiet cove,
a favorite indent on the wrinkled Maryland coast
along the Miles River, where you would stop
to watch ducks and geese, an osprey hunting,
the shifting calligraphy of the reeds.

In went your ashes, sprinkled over the side
of your handsome day sailor.
Nine grandkids dropped flowers on the water.
One of your sailing buddies, who had tethered
your boat to the others, read *A Mariner's Prayer,*
probably bending your wishes.
Another slid a bottle of double malt scotch
to the muddy bottom.

Champagne all around.
So much for synagogues, churches, bone yards.

Up north where I live, an image of your big blond face
still floats, not among the stars—those cliché machines—
but in daylight over trees and water, over marble clouds.

Day by Day

I sent this prince-of-finance Mont Blanc
for a late birthday. I chose that conqueror's pen
because I heard too often a sag in your voice
when you phoned from what would be your last home.
I was glad you had your name engraved
on its heavy black barrel.

"Nothing worked for him," she said, "after his last job.
I think he was happiest down here sailing his boat
on the river. It was so sleek and low in the water,
sometimes he seemed a part of everything out there."
Sometimes.

As I write this with our Mont Blanc, not quite
my preference really, I have a sense of grasping
your strength, for you were a big man, your passionate
affections, even your jarring grandiosity
your opinions could end a conversation in any room
you entered.

Yet this can't be the end of our story.
I am learning day by day that relations
can change—even with the dead.

Britannica Days
for Peter Jacobsohn

Dear Shade,

You caught me by surprise this afternoon
in a photo I took of you, head down, reading
at your desk before the remains of an early supper—
a half-eaten sandwich, apple slices, pots of jam
and your jar of Tiger's Milk—a transplanted Berliner,
your bald head and lofty Jewish nose shine in the light
of a lamp.

At *Britannica,* you called me Poet; your leggy,
elegant assistant was Princess, a stuffy literary sort
answered to a peremptory bark, "Colonel!"

You read the *Oresteia* once a year.
Its hard glittery language cleansed your mind.
I see you jab the air with one finger, cock your head
like Groucho: "Accuracy and flow, Poet, accuracy
and flow . . . "

You came from a publishing family.
In Berlin now, students write dissertations
on the journal your father founded in the twenties.
Poor Siegfried. He went to sleep one night
at thirty-six, and didn't wake up.

As the witless strands of war gathered,
you moved with your mother to London.
More German than the Germans, she wore a monocle.

But you, enemy alien and male,
were rounded up by the Brits and herded
aboard a ship for Canada and internment.
Torpedoed in the Irish sea, you saved a boy
your mates refused to lift aboard the life raft.

For you, the Good War passed in a camp
in the Aussie Outback, where you lost all your teeth.
Some lost more.

You married another Berliner, and to the surprise
of you both, raised a handsome, athletic American son.

Praise was anathema to you.

"You're looking prosperous today, Peter."

You raise both hands before your face.
"Poet, never never vex the gods! Didn't someone say
'They kill you for their sport?'"

Still, I raise a glass of fine wine to you,
to the frightening muse of history and to Memory,
mother of all the muses.

Real Estate

How odd to look across the way and note
the Hymans, neighbors for a generation,
are gone. Strange not to see a glimmer of light
in any window as I pass by, or Ida, bent and wiry,
climbing her stoop with a bag of groceries,
or tending the doctor, neatly dressed, asleep in his chair
on the porch, his light dimmed by a succession of strokes.

I was shocked when Ida called to say she sold
the building: two stories high, smooth gray brick,
solid as a bank. Then, one day, the big truck came.
Thirty years gone. Just like that.

We Looked at Each Other on Car 22

CALL ME! 332-2451

So many miss their stop.

Many who reach it taste
ashes and catastrophe.

Some who might have soared a little
travel parallel lines all their lives
just out of sight of each other.

So, young woman, for such a suitor,
who like Spiderman crawled across
a freshly painted wall six stories high
to scrawl his love letter to you,

why not take the chance
he aims so pointedly at you
and like Wonder Woman,
be bold, but wary.

Graduation

in memory of Peter Grattan

It was a cold spring, rain falling day after day
in my college town. When the rain stopped,
lawns were stippled with green,
the trees held up new leaves.

He opened the door of his apartment
in a white frame house above Lake Seneca,
his rooms filled with light flooding
through tall French windows.

I often came to visit that last year to hear him talk
of poets and writers, of Donne's "great entrances":
At the round earth's imagined corners, blow
Your trumpets, Angells . . .
of Finnegan's world, and Edward Lear.

One winter day he read Woolf's "The Mark on the Wall."
—That's where she found her voice—he said
and I fell in love with her quicksilvery sentences.

There was something quick about Peter, too, and daring,
and something temporary. Like my classmates and me,
he was passing through.

There was talk of a failing second marriage,
rumors he would not be granted tenure,
hints of a peripatetic life.

I had come to say goodbye
to one of my fathers,
yet had little for him but a temporary
kind of friendship.

He had a gift for me. In an old Modern Library copy
of *To the Lighthouse*, with the gold man leaping
across the cover, he wrote

> *The last day at 731 South Main,*
> *to remind you wherever you go*

Once in a While

Mother was agitated all morning.
A call had come from her brother Harold,
who was spoken of only in whispers
and despised by those with a talent
for never changing their minds.
But Mother loved him.

Somehow I learned that my uncle
had forged checks and spent time in prison.
And I knew he played the saxophone
in small jazz bands.

In late afternoon the doorbell rang.

My uncle stood in the hall.
A tall man slightly stooped, he shook snow
from his long brown overcoat. He had a high
hooked nose and wavy brown hair
that fell across his forehead,
and he carried packages wrapped in Christmas paper.

My stepfather signaled: disappear.

In early evening Uncle Harold
knocked on my door with a gift for me:
jazz records, the first I'd seen.

Fats Waller beaming from the album cover
is clearer to me now than my uncle's face.
"I can't give you anything but love, baby."

A mourning sax backing Lee Wiley:
"Once in a while, will you give just
one little thought to me . . . "

At first light my uncle was gone,
his footprints vanishing in a fresh fall of snow.

In My Next Life

I will own a sailboat sleek
as fingers of wind
and ply the green islands
of the gulf of Maine.
In my next life I will pilot a plane,
and enjoy the light artillery
of the air as I fly to our island
and set down with aplomb
on its grass runway.
I'll be a whiz at math, master five or six
of the world's languages, write poems
strong as Frost and Milosz.
In my next life I won't wonder why
I lie awake from four till daybreak.
I'll be amiable, mostly, but large
and formidable.

I'll insist *you* be present
in my next life—and the one after that.

The Revelation

I rise in the night and encounter
a strange new scent when I turn
my head just so. At last,
a visit from the other world.

Only Mother would have the fortitude
to travel all that way. And in a pleasant mood,
to judge by the freshness and sweetness
of the scent, to tell me I have long been forgiven
and to learn I long ago forgave her.

I declare an amnesty.
Everyone, everyone is forgiven.

The Kitchen Bird

Above our stove a Persian bird
flies on a Persian tile
in a surround of stalks and flowers,
some blue like his wings,
some like his breast cinnamon-rose.
His beak is open; he stares straight up.
This is the way he greets each morning.
Singing.